Keeping Out the Noise

Keeping Out the Noise

Poems by

Katherine Edgren

© 2022 Katherine Edgren. All rights reserved.
This material may not be reproduced in any form, published,
reprinted, recorded, performed, broadcast,
rewritten or redistributed without
the explicit permission of Katherine Edgren.
All such actions are strictly prohibited by law.

Author photograph by Gregory Fox
Cover design by Shay Culligan
Cover art by Cathy Muha

ISBN: 978-1-63980-139-8

Kelsay Books
502 South 1040 East, A-119
American Fork, Utah 84003
Kelsaybooks.com

Dedicated to John, Anna, and Aaron
and to all the poets who have taught and inspired me

Acknowledgments

My thanks to the editors of the publications in which the following poems have appeared, sometimes in slightly altered forms:

Barbaric Yawp: "Chevy Pick-up"

Beer, Wine, and Other Spirits," an Anthology, by World Writers: "Martini"

Birmingham Poetry Review: "That Which is Delayed"

Caffeinated Press, Inc.'s Brewed Awakenings: "October Bike Ride on the Kal-Haven Trail," "My Husband and the Installation of the Cabin Shower"

Celestial Musings: Poems Inspired by the Night Sky, an Anthology ed, Stacy Savage: "Sputnik"

Christian Science Monitor: "Untitled," "After Vacation"

Contest Edition of Peninsula Poets: "Break-in," "Early Evening, Knutson Dam," "Crow Series"

Current Magazine: "Lunar Eclipse"

Dear America, Reflection on Race, an Anthology from the Geeky Press: "The Artist's Grandmother's Carpet Hung on the Exhibit Wall"

District Lit: "Leg Brace"

Finishing Line Press: "Reverie on the Invisible Twitch, Returning from My Morning Walk"

Light Poetry Journal: "How Hot"

Main Channel Voices: "Bobby's Bike"

Ninetenths Press: "Last Times"

Oakwood–South Dakota State: "Cabin in the Minnesota Woods," "Summer Discoveries in the Land of Birth, Bath, and Beyond"

Oracle: "How it Must Have Been"

Orchard Poetry Journal: "Out West: Should We Have Stayed at Home?"

Peninsula Poets: "Midnight Musings," "The Pelicans"

Poetry Leaves Waterford Township: "Nest"

Poetry Motel: "That Summer/Mars Summer"

Poetry Society of Michigan Journal 2015: "Ode to a Pencil/Owed to a Pencil"

Poetry Society of Michigan Anthology 2016: "Reverie on the Invisible Twitch"

Poetry Society of Michigan Anthology 2020: "Petoskey Stones"

Poetry Society of Michigan Members' Journal 2020: "Rehearsal," "Snow Opera"

Red Eft: "Last Day of Tai Chi," "Hike"

Rising Voices, by University Professors Press: "Arvena"

The Coe Review: "Details," "Bikes Locked"

The Evening Street Review: "The Charles Bridge"

The New Social Worker magazine: "For Whatever is to Come"

The Way to My Heart: An Anthology of Food-related Romance, edited by Kelly Jacobson: "Harry and David's Royale Riviera Pears"

Third Wednesday: "After Bad News," "April Dissonance," "Awaiting the Hatch," "Burr Riff," "Sounds"

Willawaw Journal: "Little Brown Beauty"

Writers Reading at Sweetwaters, An Anthology: "Morning on Cass Lake"

Contents

Keeping Out the Noise

Out West: Should We Have Stayed at Home?	17
Keeping out the Noise	19
Lunar Eclipse	20
All the World's Time: A Haydn Sonnet	21
Mad Duel Mashup	22
Sounds	24
After Bad News	25
Last Day of Tai Chi	26

Conjuring Bits of Change

The Charles Bridge	29
Bobby's Bike	31
Arvena	32
Coroner's Office, Memphis, 1972	33
Words Lost and Found	34
Three Black Birds	35

Letting in the Light

How Hot?	39
Harry and David's Royale Riviera Pears	40
Garden Science	42
Martini	43
Tuesday Morning	45
Moving Makes Me Smarter	46
Ode to a Pencil/Owed to a Pencil	47
Chevy Pick-up	49
Recycling in Tiananmen Square	50
Weaving Their Own Nests	51

Cursing and Rehearsing

Last Times	55
Unfinished	57
Rehearsal	58
Little Brown Beauty	59
Details	61
Midnight Musings	63
The Artist's Grandmother's Carpet Hung on the Exhibit Wall*	64
How it Must Have Been	66
That Which is Delayed and That Which Stays	68

Contemplating While Waiting

Leg Brace	71
Prescription for a Broken Leg	73
A Prayer of Thanks for Milestones	74

Escaping to the Woods and the Lake

Break-in	77
Cabin in the Minnesota Woods	78
Morning on Cass Lake	80
The Pine Table at the Cabin	81
Reverie on the Invisible Twitch	83
Morning	86
Cabin Rhythms in the Chippewa National Forest	87
Early Evening, Knutson Dam	89
Rain	90
Summer Discoveries in the Land of Bird, Bath, and Beyond	91
Two Haiku	92
After Vacation	93

Collecting and Connecting

April Dissonance	97
More Than We'll Ever Need	98
Returning from my Morning Walk	99
Awaiting the Hatch	100
The Pelicans	101
Crows	103
Untitled	105
Nest	106
Petoskey Stones	107
October Bike Ride on the Kal-Haven Trail	109
Meditations on Naming: A Series	110
Hike	113
Snow Opera	114

Igniting Memory

Sputnik	117
Proof	118
Frailty	119
Rhubarb Days	121
Mars Summer	122

Hanging On

Bikes Locked	127
Bounty	128
My Husband, and the Installation of the Cabin Shower	129
Burr Riff	130
What Holds	131
For Whatever is to Come	132

Keeping Out the Noise

Out West: Should We Have Stayed at Home?

—inspired by E. Bishop's *Questions of Travel*

There are too many Stone People here
        standing at attention in crowded canyons
in wait for the sun to hurry up and rise or set.
        Here, striped spires born of erosion jab the sky,
while the canyon edge keeps moving back,
        and if it keeps travelling travelling,
structures on top will come to resemble ruined cities
        until the hoodoos crumble, the canyon vanishes.
There are too many layers here,
        where minerals hidden inside rocks drip like paint,
adhere to a canvas fashioned by iron, shadows, time.

The trip here, spending the night in Vegas,
        the cramped plane ride back.
Should we have stayed at home to leaf through magazines,
        surf the internet, or watch a documentary on tv?
Should we have stayed there, and thought of here?
        Where would we be today?
What compels us to leave our beds to see the sun?
        To leave recliners to hike mountains in the heat,
risk limbs for views?

Was it to see dry gullies where water once ran,
        or the way tree bark can run circles around a tree?
Was it to see a bobcat slinking through the underbrush like a ghost,
        to nearly stumble on a tarantula?
Do we have room in us for one more pink sunrise,
        one more golden sunset, one more crannied rock?

Surely, it would have been a pity to miss the opera singer
        who twirled table to table taking orders;
never to have wielded, and come to cherish, a walking stick.
        Yes, a pity not to have watched a monsoon move

over the canyon rim while sipping a local brew,
     never to have seen fearless deer with wide antenna ears, and vicious squirrels famous for attacking,
     a pity never to have been up so high we could know what it is to be a condor, or a god.
     A pity never to have been rained out from a hike to find a "sudden golden silence" in which this traveler could wonder:
     Where is home, anyway?

Keeping out the Noise

I'm writing little poems about cats—
      earplugs to keep out the noise
of a friend's recent diagnosis.
      Swat that loud cloud of hatched gnats.

Instead of visiting a failing friend,
      I'm reading novels, watching noir films.
Stories are safer to hear miles away.
      Up close, I'd see myself nearing the end.

In the *New York Times,* I turn to the Social Q's
      instead of the Sunday op-eds
or the latest Week in Review.
      Not needing another point of view.

New Yorker cartoons are more amusing
      than articles. It's more fun, less bland,
to scan the latest antics of the royal family
      than any news of Afghanistan.

Words with Friends and the Spelling Bee
      use up mental energy for
scribbling letters to reps on climate,
      the New Deal that once was Green.

I cover my eyes to keep out the noise,
      ignore the nudges as I turn away,
pull on earmuffs for decibel defense
      muffle the roars of grief and pain.

Lunar Eclipse

The dog knows we're odd.
I make popcorn.
You get your binoculars.
I take pictures of the moon as it changes.

We sit on the deck at night
and reflect on reflections—
the Moon reflecting off the Earth,
reflecting off the Sun (or something like that).

We talk about the changing colors and wonder
at all the other people watching at the same time,
and think about it just getting dark in Seattle, and how
Costa Rica is the same longitude as ours, only two hours earlier.

Contrails shine and drift across the eclipsing Moon
and all the airplanes are a part of the spectacle,
blinking white, green, and red.

Grateful for the ability of scientists to predict
this stellar event to the microsecond,
we christen the stars that appear
as the Earth's shadow tucks in the light.

All the World's Time: A Haydn Sonnet

When untitled radio music made her smile,
she knew it had to be Haydn.
Amadeus' friend, Ludwig's teacher awhile,
prolific, balletic Haydn.
Sonata or symphony, always with a measured pace
unfolded to glossy wood floors swept by long gowns,
sent out melodies widening any cramped space
lifting chin and chest, improving posture with sound
coming from entwining instruments played without duress.
Something about these gracious, spacious tunes
uncovered her hidden happiness,
granted a vantage point of high-ceiling ballrooms.
Listening to Haydn gave her all the world's time.
Time balanced, time elegant, time refined.

Mad Duel Mashup

It's a Whole Lotta Love
versus the Fifth—
Zeppelin and Beethoven
in a mad duel for who's best.
Cellists weave melodies
—one white-wigged duo
in puffy shirts, the other
in chocolate brown leather,
each pair picking up
the other's tossed gauntlet
to run a cadence of dare, defy.
Muscled arms parry bows,
sweep strings, exalt forte,
press and scrub so hard
half the horsehair hangs
dangling from the sticks
swishing away any would-be pest
with no pause for ripping,
pine scented rosin dusting the air.
Leaning in, butts off chairs,
galloping, legs squeeze
out double stops, triple stops,
climb the hills of chords.
Between spotlights strobing
in sensurround, a bow
clenched in teeth, a cello belly
thumped like a drum. Now—
not mere cellos, but galvanic—
Strats and Tele's hammering
two notes for every one,
high-pitched string noises
find overtones, bend
notes—smearing—shredding—wailing,

frenzied fingers run up and down
frets and necks lighting mayhem's fuses,
and it's Paige, Clapton, Van Halen, Hendrix
blended like good whiskey,
quadrupling brilliance.

Sounds

Betray:
how can such a treacherous word
 leave the mouth so beautifully?

After Bad News

Steep in it. Let it grow more and more astringent.
Watch it thicken, gather richness and consistency,
then sit with it until it boils over or away.

Sit with it like hunger: you won't expire.
Sit with it like thirst: you won't faint.
Sit with it the way you'd sit with a child with a tummy ache.

Sit with it like a scar that fades but never vanishes,
like joint pain when a storm is coming, or
when what's broken takes its own sweet time to heal.
Even when it scrapes and hollows you out, sit with it.

Sit with it the way the old sufferers did,
practicing patience instead of panic.
Consider randomness, confront chaos,
vines draping shoulders like a mourning shawl.

Sit with the shame of it.
Without plotting revenge, sit with it and be curious.
Sit with it and forgive.
Sit with it the way you sit with someone
when there's nothing left to say.

Practically speaking, if you don't sit with it,
it will sit on you, wake you in the small hours.
If you need to, tell yourself it has great potential.
If you need to, tell yourself there's beauty in it.

Sit with it like the bud of an idea, and see if it blooms.
Open your fist, hold its hand.
Sit with it until you believe it.
Because every bit of what you sit with
is your precious life.

Last Day of Tai Chi

We'd learned thirty poses together,
practiced balancing, slowing breath,
searched synapses for the next pose,
as we slowly moved our bodies in
graceful choreography.

Forming our usual circle to close—
arms-width apart, feet together,
we relaxed our faces with a smile,
the warrior, arm bent, fist on the right
the scholar, arm bent, flat hand on the left,
then joined hands in front of hearts
before bowing first to the front—to everyone—
then to a neighbor on one side, then the other.
I felt a twinge that it was over—
this group, this teacher, this mirrored room,
Thursday afternoons from 1–2.

After all the stepping backward, forward,
gathering with our arms, lifting legs to corner-kick,
patting the horse's mane, grasping the bird's tail,
carrying the yoke, picking up needle from sea-bottom,
chopping through mountain, making cloud hands,
we were ending
in the same spot where we began.

Conjuring Bits of Change

The Charles Bridge

Prague, Christmas 2006

In 1357, they stirred egg yolks into mortar
to give strength to this stone bridge that still stands.
Along the sides they lifted up sculptures,
now blackened by time,
to form a statue alley of saints and martyrs
that watch over all who cross
or gaze out upon the silver Vltava:
all the water colorists hawking souvenir art,
the caricaturists, tourists,
and musicians with guitar cases open,
who sing and play in oases of sound.

Amidst the iconic bustle
is one of the beggars of Praha.
His dirty, rag-worn back
contorts into submission,
as close to the ground as he can get,
as if we who cross
are royalty. Asking without words
he conjures bits of change.
He holds his position for hours
like a frozen statue, or someone
already dead.

In all the history of this ancient structure
that connects older town to new,
and saints and martyrs to beggars,
neither church, art,
nor commerce have found a way
to bridge the empty expanse
between the living martyr
and the rest of us. His humanity alone
does not fill his case with crowns.

My hands are cold in their gloves.
I see his trembling, upturned palm.

Bobby's Bike

The weatherman predicts a low of minus 6,
the heart of winter. It is now just getting dark.
Black clouds drift in.

Driving home in my mini-van after my $52 haircut,
I see Bobby, who slowly climbs onto his bike,
leaving the Day Shelter after another long day,
talking to himself. He looks worse than last time.
His ruddy cheeks puff and sag.

He's wearing that same old ex-yellow coat,
at least he has a warm hat and gloves.
I have an urge to stop the car and say, *Hey Bobby,
get in* and bring him home for a nice meal,
a good bath, a warm bed in the guest room.

Once I found a collage he made and abandoned
in the dumpster. Little pieces of photographs and words
cut out of magazines, pieces of a broken mirror,
all glued strategically, preserved and framed.

He avoids the Night Shelter as if it were a jail.
He has a sleeping bag hidden in the woods near the railroad tracks.

Arvena

Jailed for her mental illness:
profound, un-regulate-able.

They couldn't decide what to do with her
ranting on the streets.

When she couldn't breathe
she begged for her medicine

but they refused to listen
to the ravings of a lunatic—

saw no need to check her fat chart to see
if her condition warranted medicine.

This time they were wrong
and she was,

unfortunately,
correct.

In cardiac arrest when they found her,
face blue, airway clenched,

and no amount of wishing could revive a mind
stirred to composing cartoons, dance steps, songs.

After she was gone, her family sued.

It wasn't the jail's guilt the lawyers disagreed about,
but the monetary value to place on a life so full of temper.

Coroner's Office, Memphis, 1972

Every afternoon, I'd steel myself
before shuffling through the Polaroid stack
left on my desk corner for filing:
dead bodies from the day before. Evil rashes
of shotgun wounds, the surprised eyes of those
who knew they were goners glaring back at me.
Drownings—bodies puffed up like small whales,
suicides by gun to mouth or head.
I am still haunted by the wild eyes
of the speed addict who OD'd in the closet,
and by the thick, Ascaris worms crawling out
of the orifices of children as they cooled—
children who had played in a parasite-laced sandbox
in this city of neglect and despair.

Words Lost and Found

They've put us in the Garden Cottage
at the Bayview B & B, built as a hotel in 1911.
Our room was once an ice cream parlor.
Four red, plastic stools still swivel at the counter.
I spin on one after the long drive, and it takes me back
to Woolworth's, to Detroit, and to Viktor,
a man I visited Fridays as a part of a college psych class.

He'd spent many silent years
in the back wards of Ypsi State Hospital.
I'd find him sitting mute in a dark corner
of the group home he'd been released to
next to an elderly female resident
clutching a doll to her breast.

Somewhere along the way, Viktor had lost his language,
but still loved reading the words of others.
He and I would bus to the library for books.
Afterwards, we'd head to Woolworths for thick malts.
Sitting together on the red stools, I'd watch his
nicotine-stained fingers hand-roll a cigarette.

Even though returned to the outside world,
Viktor continued to keep his own counsel.
I, on the other hand,
filled the quiet spaces with my chatter.

I didn't know his story, and he wasn't telling,
though I remember one yellow afternoon
walking to the bus stop
he awarded me the words: *What a beautiful day!*

Three Black Birds

Three black birds with thick bodies
fold their wide wings to take a stand
in the arthritic branches of March's burr oak:
turkey vultures. Castaneda wrote that
three black birds portend death.

But these are Shakespeare's witches,
stirring a smoky cauldron in their
blood-soaked brains
as we defy them with so much life.

Letting in the Light

How Hot?

It's so hot this hen won't lay.
      She'll hold her eggs for a cooler day.
But when she lets them go at last
      they'll turn rotten very fast.

It's so hot this dog won't walk,
      just a short one, then she'll balk,
flop in cool grass in the shade,
      while Mama longs for lemonade.

It's sizzling hot all over town.
      So hot the grass is blanching brown.
It stabs your butt, so you can't sit.
      Are we in drought? No doubt of it.

Harry and David's Royale Riviera Pears

*After years of study, scientists discovered
pears are best eaten naked, in the bath,
their juices streaming down.*

They came in the mail.
As per pear instructions,
we waited—only two days—
and they were ready. Predictable. Un-fickle.

Their best time is narrow,
blessed with a perfect moment of just-ripeness.
Vigilance is required to discern the moment in its thinness.
It's best when it all comes together—texture, flavor,
when just the right notes sing.

Each day remembering to check back,
to open the dark box resting on the counter
and fingertip-test, where the stem joins the fruit—
the fontanel of the pear.

Such fleeting perfection,
each pear joins the society of others with too-short lives—
the mayfly, the day lily, the evening primrose.

So cool and sweet, so white-fleshed and plush;
good thin-sliced, with alternating bites
of sharp white cheddar on a fresh plate,
juicy snowflakes drifting outside.

The pears are voluptuous.
Dimpled, they blush and turn,
open and open again.
The cool shell softens, lingers.
And like love, there's ripening, yielding.

We both inhale.
Our hands, mouths, tongues, lips
find, nibble, bite, catch
the succulence, as we abandon ourselves
to the sweetness of submission.

Garden Science

Spinning her own experiments
while missing courtroom conflict,
the retired lawyer
sets aggressive native plants
next to each other,
letting them duke it out.
Her husband likes order—
alphabetizes the spice cabinet—
but she prefers the tussle of the unknown,
the discovery of who's fittest,
who will go down for the count,
who will survive.

Martini

I like to sit with E.B. White's *elixir of quietude*
at the end of a hard day, but

I prefer mine classic—
straight up with an olive. Never dirty.

And *please* do not stuff the olive with anything
other than the pimento it was born with.

(Though sometimes I desire the kiss
of a twisted lemon.)

Depending on mood,
I'll take either vodka or gin

with a whisper of vermouth:
think vermouth over the glass, or

look at it across the room,
the way Churchill liked to do.

The vodka must be *Grey Goose* or *Absolut* or
Skyy in the electric blue bottle,

but I'm not fussy about the gin.
Bombay Sapphire or *Tanqueray*. Something smooth.

Don't let Mencken's *only American invention as perfect
as the sonnet* languish in the shaker diluting,

losing its crisp astringent essence;
and never call it a vodkatini or kangaroo.

"Martini" is not a synonym for cocktail. It is not sweet.
It is not an apple, chocolate or pineapple-tini

Don't add liqueur or sugar or champagne.
Don't turn it into a bubbly girly drink.

Don't ever think it deserves the name *martini*
if it's orange or pink.

Let's raise a martini toast, dear love!

Tuesday Morning

Popples popples popples/pines pines pines/ birches birches birches

Bracken ferns/vetch/rue/Queen Anne's lace

Me riding my bike down the road/Me riding my bike down the road

Bracken ferns/vetch/rue/Queen Anne's lace – a bunny!

Popples popples popples/pines pines pines/ birches birches birches

Moving Makes Me Smarter

Stretched limbs unlock stiff ice,
pound a sluggish heart,
nudging blood that's sludgy
to leaping hurdles, making art.

Blood that's circulating
jolts stray thoughts
into percolating:
moving makes me smarter.

Jiggling brain cells, juggling
puzzles, woken neurons risen so high
look for ways out, bubbling
aha! oh me! oh my!

Making tracks from usual
piques insight, tweaks anomie,
coming nose to nose with original
outs nuance, cracks complexity.

Moving to move,
donning layer upon layer
is a workout in itself,
deep in winter's groove.

Moving makes me smarter,
oils a spine from neck to tailbone
lubes joints so pain and stiffness
won't distract, disgorge a groan.

Without moving I will drowse,
how to get sharp with eyes shut,
longing to be aroused?
It's moving that makes me smarter.

Ode to a Pencil/Owed to a Pencil

Not to put too fine a point on it, but the pen
is secretive, holds everything inside.
Treacherous, perhaps even malevolent,
its innards can explode, leak,
and stain your shirt and hands with ink.
And while the pen is mightier than the sword,
sometimes it's unreliable. Grab a Biro,
or a Bic Clic Stic when you need it
and it can easily fail you.
Burying a dead pen can be satisfying.
Pens that can't be revived with a scribble
should be tossed without a quibble.

Some may praise the pen's symmetry,
the color of ink, width of tip,
but it's the pencil that's dependable
since they carried Ticonderogas in the Conestogas,
and it still offers degrees of hardness and softness.
The pencil is frequently yellow, hexagonal
for a good grip, and consistently asserts
the color of its core with bold, sharp marks.
While most pens recognize only permanence,
a pencil recognizes fallibility,
and is prepared to be helpful.
It understands the virtue of humility.

Pencils are trustworthy.
You can tell merely by looking whether it'll work.
Leave one in a drawer for years, and it never quits.
A pencil is faithful, stoic, easily forgotten, under-appreciated,
and yet performs! Oh, the point can break
or it can grow dull, but a pencil can be made sharp again.

It's true that eventually it becomes a stub,
but only after a long life
giving of its very marrow.

Chevy Pick-up

Macho woman forked over fifty bucks for me in '73.
      Rode way up high like a trucker,
changed my oil when she was feelin' low.

Check the side-mirror. I'm glow-in-the-dark blue, crayola blue.
      Yellow shag on walls and floor once was new,
sagging bucket seats too.

I'm clunky, clattery, but automatic. Radio works.
      Shocks pretty bad.
Take those corners real slow…

Rusty door not always reliable.
      Try the passenger side, girl!
Winters, sometimes both doors. Windows too.

HONK HONK HONK!
      We'd yell, she'd bang on the window
and hope for some kind passer-by.

Summers, she took me on spins for ice cream
      my windows down, her long hair flyin',
radio blasting Clapton, Hendrix, Led Zeppelin.

She'd shove a mattress into my hard bed
      and take the whole gang and their younguns'
to fireworks on the 4th of July

She sold me for seventy-five bucks in '75.
      Worth every penny.

Recycling in Tiananmen Square

The line to Mao's body snakes through the *Gate of Heavenly Peace*. The 109-acre plaza swarms with visitors,
including pilgrims from rural China.

Moving slowly in line, under Mao's looming portrait,
we foreign tourists find distraction watching toddlers squatting,
making puddles on the pavement. Speakers blare patriotic music.

Surveillance cameras are affixed to high poles in every direction.
We're supposed to keep any questions about the violent,
repressive history of this space to ourselves.

Vendors sell large bouquets of flowers for tributes to Mao,
his embalmed body on display since his death in 1976
"fluffed up" on a regular basis to dispel noticeable decomposition.

When we enter the mausoleum we're directed to maintain solemn
faces: no speaking or laughing. It's a strain to control our
emotions. Many of us have never seen a dead body before.

As we slowly walk by the glass case, we see masses of flower
tributes from visitors. Leaving, we see a worker hastily collecting
the bouquets, returning them to the vendors, for resale.

Weaving Their Own Nests

The one who loves to hear herself talk.
The one whose politics I don't dare ask about.
The one so shy, he prefers to be alone.
The one who's crazy about cats.
The one who, when I whistle, whistles back.

The blue one who forgets what he committed himself to.
The young one who isn't permitted to go anywhere
because of her mother. Her mother.
The one I haven't seen in a year, in hiding.

All the perfectionists, the preeners.
The brilliant pair who care excessively what others think.
The other pair, busy all the time,
or who knows what would happen?
The scattered ones who plan to get organized:

like birds with their singular natures,
habits, habitats, and migrating patterns,
with all their varied trills and whistles
weaving their quirky nests.

Cursing and Rehearsing

Last Times

Breaking track in the shelter of fragrant pines
is over for us. Our knees and hips protest.
Instead of storing skis and poles forever,
we donate them to a resale shop.
The last time had come and gone.

You always know the first time,
but rarely see the last one coming. Afterwards,
in the rearview mirror, you glimpse
the fork in the road, that eternal detour,
as you hear the clunk of the curtain's fall.

Your parents pick you up and set you down so many times,
and being carried is like riding an elephant,
an enormous luxury. Eventually,
you grow big or heavy, too self-sufficient,
or want to go faster, and they stop.

So many last times: the last warm day, last snow,
last menstrual blood. Pre-pandemic,
the last time soaking in a hot tub filled with chatty women,
the last time I sang beside others,
the last feeling of safety.

The last time I saw my brother, now a stranger.
The last time I saw my mother. Her powdery pink skin,
thin bones visible beneath. The look of desperation
I wasn't able to erase.
The last time I saw clearly, before eye surgery,
or slept without pain.

What would be different if I knew it was the last time
we'd wake together in the same bed?
Would I try to say something wise?
Say thank you? Apologize?

Unfinished

Our lives end littered with unfinished narratives,
un-raked leaves, a messy garden,
tomatoes left to rot on the vine.

Episodes are felled like trees, split like logs.
Logical extensions are edited out,
amendments or addendums discontinued,
as all the plot lines shrink.

Artists who leave drafts and sketches,
fizzled bursts of inspirations,
broad washes, mixed shades, and storied,
stored canvasses that never made it to the frame

are interrupted by a vagrant breeze
ripping the brush from their hands,
leaving the arc's curve to be drawn by others.

The still life we paint is partial,
incomplete, opaque, inchoate,
the opposite of pat or neat,
despite the richness of the colors,
and any lucky capture of the light.

Some mercies are never granted,
farewells never said.
All bewilderment, any guesses,
any once-imagined resolutions,
are tossed into the air like confetti,
carried away by the annihilating wind.

Rehearsal

Waking, I place fingertips on the pulse of night and day,
dark and light and see: there is still time and life.

Resurrected, I can dismiss or confront glimpses granted:
dancing in the arms of those who've gone,

flying, diving, swimming with giant fish,
watching teeth crumble, listening to

talking babies wearing dirty diapers,
steering cars without brakes over flooding roads.

I can stare at morning's clean page, or sense
coiled springs in a body longing to be soft.

Then too, there are mornings I can't recall
what or whether I dreamt; only certain that sleep

was like chocolate: deep, dark, delicious
in this nightly rehearsal,

this sliver of oblivion, this toe-dip, this
chance to ask: was the void so bad?

Death's always clanging counterpoint
beneath a too-short, waking life.

Little Brown Beauty

Inspired by "Window Strike Series, Little Brown Beauty II,"
—a watercolor by Valerie Mann

Why rush the kitchen window every morning
to bang your tender head upon the glass?

Experts declare: "protecting territory."
That interloper has got to go,
and you're just the soldier to do it,
a troop of one, your life's quixotic business.

I've plastered the window with post-it notes,
tried closing the shade, but you simply choose
another window.
                I admire your persistence,
wonder at futility
                see how you're like me.

One day, I find your body beneath the window,
neck broken, twitching forever stilled,
subdued enough for a watercolorist.

Wrapped in plain, brown stripes,
from a family too abundant to be rare.
One of a long, undistinguished series

showing what can happen when you chase away
the one who looks like you, charge forward
instead of stepping back,
                the fallibility of instinct.

Along with your mussed, lumpy chest, your
cunning beak, and your already desiccating carcass,
your feet are what will stick with me:
curved, wiry offerings to the morning sky.

Details

They start out so small,
insignificant,
subordinate.

Trifles, dots, jots,
flecks, iotas, tittles,
scraps, snippets.

Only minim.
Feeble, puny,
meager.

But stubborn like a stain.

Mud-rollers in the daytime,
at night, they turn into slippery, devilish imps
who hide around corners, and

leap out to startle
with googley eyes and dripping tongues.

Greedy feeders on haste and forgetfulness,
they grow fat and fatter,
until they are obese, imposing,

then march their muddy feet
all over what you thought
was nearly done.

They leave wide wakes of humiliation and regret.
They make you mistaken,
require apologies,

force you to rope and corral them,
break and smooth their rough edges,
and de-tail them,

detach their heads from their necks and
de-liver them with delight, diced and cut,
into the smallness of their little souls.

Midnight Musings

I've been trying to envision what it's like in heaven
now that Mom's gone, her second husband following
four months later. Will there be a grand reunion?
Will it be awkward? He was getting kind of tired
of her toward the end. We're talking eternity here.

Had she already joined up with Dad
who departed suddenly, twenty-one years ago?
Will the two of them welcome her second husband,
Dad thanking him for looking out for her so well?
Or will her second husband prefer to catch up

with his first wife, my mother's cousin?
Maybe Dad will have found some chicky,
and prefer not to be bothered with his wife
of over 40 years. The whole thing
seems kind of messy to me.

Will the body's joys be forgotten or stirred up,
or will they have bodies at all? Perhaps monogamy
will be forsaken, the moment of death erasing
earthly thoughts, creating a kind of amnesia

even about boundaries among people
and they'll all become one singing, shining soul,
a choir of angels, one bright star,
a synchrony of birds, flocking.

The Artist's Grandmother's Carpet Hung on the Exhibit Wall*

I see him
peeling carpet from wood floor, rolling it up,
    with a plan to display this relic like a quilt,
top to ceiling, folded where it touches the floor.

This carpet-artist asks me to consider
mundane objects as art.

Dish-water beige, wearing dirt stains, remnants
of muddy feet, souvenirs of coming and going,
entrances and exits,
drinkers of coffee or tea. Perhaps a dog.

Carpet as detritus, carpet as life-witness.
Well-worn rug, well-worn grandmother,
who may have tried to clean it,
    or maybe carpet stains were the least of her concerns.

There to keep her feet from touching cold,
for softening the jar, preventing the slip and hard fall.

He liked to visit Grandmother's house.
The carpet means home,
and he wants to preserve a piece of it, or

he never noticed the carpet until she died,
spending attention on the woman herself, or

he neglected to visit at all,
and didn't see the carpet until it
    was all that was left.

The carpet is loneliness.
The carpet is regret,
gray sky, horizon of grief.

* The artist was Rodney McMillian, and his art work, "Untitled." The exhibit was called 30 Americans, and was meant to be an eye-opener on the black experience. At the Detroit Institute of the Arts, January 2016.

How it Must Have Been

He runs to escape what he cannot have.
Growing tired, he slows to a walk,
chances on the railroad track—
and turns left, as he would.

He follows the empty track
into the moonless night,
with the same cold bars to plod between,
the flat ladder going nowhere

and there is no change, the same
cold monotony, too endless to think.
He sinks into numbness,
the edge of sleep.

He sits on the rail to rest, feels
the night's breath on his curved back,
and looks up to meet
the cold eyes of the incoherent sky.

He digs out the last cigarette from the pack,
feels the bitter warmth in his chest,
the way it drifts into his lungs.
Exhaling, he watches the thin smoke vanish

and for a moment he's glad he kept smoking
despite the naysayers, because it turns out he was right,
there was no need
to preserve himself for old age.

The subliminal thunder of the train
intrudes upon his empty silence.
Louder and louder, closer and closer,
and he thinks: *Why not?*

He doesn't need to steel himself.
This will be so easy.
He closes his eyes
and takes a long deep breath.

That Which is Delayed and That Which Stays

efflorescence of stars
just now reaching eyes;
the boat's hum, heard under water,
the man in the canyon at sunrise—

swing chop pause, the cleft wood-sound,
suspense of the notched, steered
oak, last splendor found
the same way thunder follows light

and the sluggish nerve
that carries bad news to the brain,
and shock
that holds to itself the pain

or bone or mark, scar or stain
the common hollowness that contains
a muted fragrance
within a silence

and stillness filled, complete
with quiet reverberation of grief
with no way to explain
that which follows and remains

Contemplating While Waiting

Leg Brace

My brace encases my leg
the way a spun cocoon embraces a caterpillar.
I wait months for the hatching, to fly in long strides.

> *Oh to chase and be chased again!*

I dream of getting up from my chair and walking away.

> *I remember walking.*

Instead, I've plenty of time to contemplate a brace,
as I hang upside down from an un-steady thread,
twirling in the breeze.

My brace holds my leg in an inanimate state,
lulls it into a long sleep—a Snow White trance,
as it waits for the waking kiss.

My brace distinguishes my leg from all my other parts,
makes me look as if I stepped out of *Clockwork Orange*,
or the *Bionic Woman*.

This black python constricts from ankle to hip.

My brace prevents jiggling and sagging.
A black bra for my leg.

> *I'd rather go bra-less.*

My brace is a darkroom with something developing inside,
where unused muscles shrink, skin sheds,
where there's a pink, hot leg above a prickly, swelling foot.

When I take it off for a bath, my brace
is a six-legged octopus I'm trying to tame—
straps flying around, sticking to themselves and each other.

At last, the time done,
I'll move and shake my leg, do the wake up dance
with two clashing fancies:
burn it, or
        kiss it.

Prescription for a Broken Leg

Take a dose of dog-lick spit, soak up a doggy stare,
knead a hairy belly.

Whisk with a glance of fox stealing into the drain pipe.
Let the linden's reds and pale frost seal it in.

Alternate between feeling like a tea bag steeping in a hot bath,
and a numbed fish on ice.

Let any errant pain be tickled by the absurdity of *Portlandia,*
or relaxed by a panoply of Bach tracks on the player.

Lounge on the porch like *Hans Castorp,* sun flooding
your face, knowing your trajectory is up.

Savor comfort food and launch the goods to every cell.
A tincture of martini will return you to yourself.

Wrestle with balms of strap and Theraband;
touch toe to ground, once granted poise and balance.

Lend your voice to ascend in a community of song,
and let the needles of vibration mend you

along with tender touch,
and ample time.

A Prayer of Thanks for Milestones

Sitting at the table to eat,
pulling on socks,
doing up my brace nice and tight,
managing stairs,
wearing shoes,
toe-touching,
sleeping on my side,
driving,
pain lifting like fog,
the first shower,
the first bath,
the first wine, first martini, first scotch
the last of the narcotics, stool-softeners,

while all the time, unseen, underground:
knitting, purling, weaving, soldering, gluing.

Mending.
Amen.

Escaping to the Woods and the Lake

Break-in

Thieves smashed the pane of glass
closest to the door lock
leaving strewn crystals of glass
on the Welcome mat,
despite our careful placement
of only two nails.
(All they had to do was
remove the nails
and lift out the glass.
No finesse in these thieves.)

We look to see what's missing,
we had left nothing to steal—
TV, old tools, long gone.

Assembling our first meal, I am
unaccustomed to the homes
of all the implements.
Each time I can't find something—
pan lid, coffee pot, big spoon,
I think *it's because it's been stolen.*
Petty thieves, indeed.

And the kitchen chairs seem
rearranged. What did they do,
play pinochle?

Cabin in the Minnesota Woods

I can name mouse tracks on the road after rain.
I know the lobster mushroom, the purple aster,
campion, columbine, and wild artichoke.
I can find wolf milk slime on decaying logs.
Facing wildness every day, I let it stir me,
though I can never truly understand.

Eagles hail me as I glide along their shore,
accustomed to me as I to them; even mottled ones,
before they earn their heads and tails of white.
Here, like my dog, I'm free to run or sit,
sleep or wake when and where I wish.

I've seen all the shapes and colors clouds take.
I've watched the sun's slow journey west
at the coming equinox, the tilt of Earth
imaginable and tangible, at this latitude.
I've heard the continuum of wind: the Heathcliff
kind that renders breathlessness, and the lack of it
permitting kayaking along the shore,
peering at what's deep and clear.
Having lost power from a downed tree,
I've come to wholly appreciate electricity.

This is the place I've come hurt or picked up hurt:
a tooth, a foot, a leg, an eye, my old war wounds.
Here, I've grown intimate with pain, and found
forgiveness that sometimes accompanies healing,
and I've rarely known insomnia in days so full
tumbling into oblivion is easy.

Here I put myself in the open face of awe,
and build my life upon its rock, possessing
knowledge that is sedimentary, layered

with years before, years still with me. This
is where I know the drop-offs where fish gather,
where I spy merganser, kingfisher, pelican.
This is where—hearing the voice of the loon—
I've scattered ashes, remembering all those lost to me.

I've sat by woodstove fires for warmth and illumination.
I've known the cast of light at sunrise, the sweep and rush
in just one day, patience that's deep, and how to love
what changes, the thread of transience stitching into me.

Morning on Cass Lake

My wrists trace figure eights in the bug-free air.
The kayak grants me long arms, a long glide.
I dip and pull through shallows and dappling shadows,
widening rings of minnows scattering,
vortices drawn by skittering water striders.
Wild rice glistens beyond the reeds.

Beyond Buck's, past the tall pines, close to shore,
there's a short cry, a stirring. The eagle apparates
like a cross pinned to sky—white head and tail,
dark body piercing the cosmic blue.

Good morning, old pajama wearer, Minnesota denizen,
thermal hanger, with your wings that tilt and hold.
For seconds we levitate. Air and water bind us,
as life widens and skitters and glistens.

The Pine Table at the Cabin

Back in the 50's when I was in elementary school,
John's Dad built a cabin, and a table for the cabin,
with tapered legs constructed of two pieces of wood
set at right angles, bolted together, then fastened to a tabletop
plastered with fake-brick, glued-on linoleum.
Next to the wood stove, always absorbing
the perfume of morning fires, laden with

a cordless power drill with charger—for installing a shower: at last!
Two packages of *Tred-not* deerfly patches—for next year's plague.
Earplugs in a hot pink bubblegum case—for when we mow the lawn.
A big spindle of sisal baler twine that will last for the rest of our
    lives.
A yoga strap, in case we're inspired.
Three red and white bobbers. They didn't bring luck.
Four legs from a couch that was finally pitched.
Some found string all balled up—you never know.
Ten nails, some new, some bent.
A yellow box of (I'm told) Allen wrenches.
A magnifying glass for inspecting insects or bat skeletons up close.
A green screen door handle that's been replaced,
and could be tossed, except it was used by John's parents.
A piece of red linoleum broken off from the kitchen counter,
set there by John's Dad.
Light bulbs for flashlights to find our way to the cabin from the
lake after fishing, or in case there's a power outage.
A Beltrami County Solid Waste Management Program ID Card—
in case they ask for it (they never have) at the dump/transfer station.

A Brochure of Itasca State Park—the headwaters of the Mississippi where we biked a seventeen mile, up-and-down trail and saw the biggest white and red pines in Minnesota.
A cup of coffee that was hot when I started this list.

Reverie on the Invisible Twitch

My fingers circle the rod in supplication
       for the quick jink of fish bite—

like hands on the Ouija board's pointer, as a child—
       I still wait for the twitch of the invisible.

But now

it's fish, not predictions, that I divine,
       as we troll gently, motor murmuring.

*

Sometimes my bait drags on bottom so weedy
       it mocks the perch bite
and tricks me into setting the hook.

A kind of electricity
       echoes up the line, tingles through the rod
and into my hands.

My dulled head blazes
       with the mystery underneath the calm.

And when a fish finally does bite,
       it is like the feet of a fetus, flutterkicking.

If the male of our species wants to know that illegible tug,
       he needs only to fish.

*

Some are timid lickers or samplers,
                               others, bold yankers and runners.

Some travel companionably in schools,
                               others are loners.

Some are ancient,
                others, too small to keep.

                *

The great Mississippi channels through the lake like a road
      carrying bizarre, giant fish on long journeys, stoking
dreams.

Perhaps there will be a fish so big it will break my line, or pull my rod
                       into the water: a Muskie—fish of a
           thousand casts!

                *

The lake is fed by fishermen
and decorated with lost lures and lines,
the smoothed branches of old trees.
We coast in the middle—sky above—water below—
three connected universes teeming with creatures.

                *

We wait for hours—doing without doing.
      Looking down, it grows too dark to see.

Flicking on running lights, we find ourselves
 just one in a twinkling community on this dark land of
water,

lungs open,
 practicing optimism, learning hope.

Morning

Rare Quiet.
Wild quiet.
Windless quiet.
Wide horizon quiet.
Bugs sleeping in grass and trees quiet.
Boy sleeping quiet.
Flicker and crow quiet.
No mowers, motors, or chain saws, quiet.
No husband snoring quiet.
No rain on the roof quiet.
No wind shaking rain off trees onto the roof quiet.
No dog licking herself quiet.
Beside me, inside me,
quiet.
Quite quiet.

Cabin Rhythms in the Chippewa National Forest

Fumble with the main fuse in the dark, trip
the septic alarm that shrieks when the power goes on,
and after a sluggish start, the water heater fires, the fridge hums,
pump impellers spin, and we can drink and wash and flush.
Cabin smells flow with wood smoke and bacon mornings
above a counterpoint of DEET, sunscreen, and calamine lotion.
We practice a hat and head-net ritual for relaxed cadences of daily
dog walks. Then there are syncopated tick-checks before bed,
with a flashlight over naked bodies.

Avoiding mosquitoes and black flies, we dance an edgy jitterbug
installing dock and boat lift, followed by the largo of lugging a
heavy motor and full gas can down to the boat—stopping to rest—
and the slow waltz of two kayaks ferried along the same steps.
After stop-and-start measures as we step the mast, our sailboat
tangos over the five-mile wide lake.
Phoebe weaves her nest beneath the eaves, dips to fresh-mown
grass, rises, dips again, and we follow her conductor's wand with
our eyes. Our eyes rest too, on the fermata of the eagle in his
nesting tree. Our ears are showered with the drumming and the
primal calls of the flicker, the downy, the pileated.

So much again and again, another and another.
The scherzo and cantabile of weather, the dissonance of rain on the
roof—all the desires that come upon us: the necessities of eating
Dave's Pizza, celebrating at *Tutto Bene* with olive soup.
We gulp down days like beer from *Bemidji Brewing.*
Even when it's gray or there are too many bugs, we wait,
knowing pauses and silences are a part of the whole.
Sometimes we break rhythm to retire early after showers,
clean and sexy between buttery sheets,
knowing the tempo will return like wildflowers—
the way one blooms and fades—silent fireworks.
Afternoons, the hammock's always creaking, evenings,

there are Happy Hours on the porch, cool breezes,
and a shimmer hovering over the lake.
Any singular stresses or agitato back home fall away
into a peace unlike any other,
as we meld into a rhythm that returns us every year,
one small part of a great, northern forest.

Early Evening, Knutson Dam

What was it that led us
on the dog's last walk of the day?

What make one of us look up and see
a scrap of gold behind a screen of clouds?

Who suggested we stay
to watch mist rise off the wetland

and hear the raucous dog
root out ducks within the reeds

as the moon heaved up like a golden mushroom
to shine a corridor upon the river?

Rain

The shriveled grass lifts spiky brown heads
to receive the rain, and what was parched plumps up.
The once-gasping ground is a living sponge.

Passionate wet lips press fern and birch, pine and poplar—
even the witchy trees, with their tangled lichen-branches—
beside rings of dimpled mushroom funnels, ready for rain.

Thirsty crows, pileated woodpeckers, owls
drowsing among forest branches lift their heads
to the trickling tonic washing over them.

Rain splashes the exposed stones of a shrinking lake,
fills it with cupful after cupful of whitest wine
until all the giddy fish turn mellow.

Deeply dreaming beneath new shingles,
I hear the roof-drum's music seep into me,
and break up all my knotted clots.

Drenched with sound,
my once-hollow bowls overflow,
safe and dry inside cabin walls.

Summer Discoveries in the Land of Bird, Bath, and Beyond

First, the molecules rush to boil.
Then the slow perk of the coffee pot,
like the sound of great waves rolling in from the lake,
and all the rushy-twittering of the leaves in the wind
that brings the smells that make the dog howl,
and a bed as hard as the floor, and
then there are all the uses of *beat:*
the drum, the wife, the cake-batter. We
walk the beat, sail the beat, beat it.
And the lyric of the bracken fern that filters sun,
and the exclamation points of the tall grasses
making a painting, Chinese.

Things pop up when we're not looking:
mushrooms, pimples, wrinkles,
freckles, warts, moles,
no-fat hotdogs, trashy magazines.

We see that fireweed burns on the side of the road,
the turtle skips on the river like a stone,
and it's the bullfrog who grunts,
the green frog who twangs.

Strange chants wake us in the early morning.
A giant bird sails over the road.
At night, the shadow in the outhouse
is made by a tiny bug on the lens of the flashlight.
The sky runs amok with rain, hammers rain,
the dog is exhausted,
and untamed, weedy eyebrows run wild and free.

Two Haiku

Sailing

Wind dies at the shore
white wings are flapping slowly.
Tired, cabbage moth.

Lake Wind

Unleashed lake-wind
makes chevrons, v-curves, choppy
sea of little breasts.

After Vacation

Reeds inhabit, then hold
the direction of the wind
as they bend toward shore.

The tiller,
the fishing pole, the handlebars
still inhabit my curled fingers.

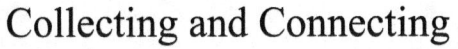
Collecting and Connecting

April Dissonance

what crazy season is this,
with flowers, like moonlight, shining in the linden
and beyond,
frost
glittering on the grass?

More Than We'll Ever Need

In spring, the pear tree is an extravaganza of blossoms,
and the forest floor is extravagant with trillium
as if to arrest our eyes.
Because extravagance arrests.

In summer, parachuting cottonwood seeds
are landing everywhere. Profligate trees insure survival,
like cotton-brained orators filling the air with words,
hoping some will stick.

In Biology Class, no one wants to dissect a female frog,
certain to be extravagantly-packed with eggs.
Needing cleaning out
before you can check for any of the other parts.

And think of the mass production of minnows!
This seems to be nature's way: profusions of blossoms,
twining vines of ivy, lavish, immoderate weeds,
hills and fields extravagant with more green than we'll ever need.

Sometimes spending freely, nature goes beyond bounds of reason:
with Canada geese and all their droppings, with every itch-trigger:
poison ivy, mosquitoes, black flies, and chiggers.
Extravagance is always plural, never singular.

Everyone needs times of extravagance
where they don't consider the cost, where
they can be free and rash, where fists can unclench,
fingers can stretch and take, which makes me ask:

What do I have plenty of to spare?
Extra is part of extravagance.
Extravagance is generous,
unearned grace.

Returning from my Morning Walk

Blinding sunrise forces my eyes down
to reveal—for the first time—
the long shadows made
by even the tiniest pebbles.

Awaiting the Hatch

Everyone was waiting for the eggs to hatch.
The way you wait for spring or summer.
      The way you wait for anything.

Would it be like waiting for Godot?
      Would our hopes be merely fond?

We'd lost track of how many weeks
she'd been sitting on them.
      Perhaps they were infertile.
At what point would the swans give up?

Together with the pen and cob,
we grew eager to greet and name the cygnets.

Walking the wetland, I snap photographs
      of the white swan puddle
on the nest of cattail stems and twigs and wonder:

had the Goose Lady with her kayak and barking dogs,
      hired to rid the grounds of geese,
provoked an unintended consequence?

The Pelicans

I can't zero in on one, the way Elizabeth does
with her Sandpiper. There's no "the pelican," only pelicans.
What's riveting is their tight crowd
on the stony breakwater, resembling rocks themselves.
So many! (A few more and they'd be menacing).
It's a Christmas morning of pelicans, a Woodstock of pelicans.
A colony. Conference. Mob. With dazzling plumage in this pod
that gleams so whitely in morning's sun—
perching, floating, fishing, scooping.

Quiet, for a crowd. With orange, pencil-colored beaks:
those wearing a beak-bump are breeding males.
Nothing subtle here. Looking for food and love.
Sharp-elbowed, with black-tipped wings,
long tufted heads, and crazy punk hairdos
resembling a forest of umbrellas hung out to dry,
closing and opening to float up like Mary Poppins
in ones, twos, threes: scouts, search parties, squadrons,
wing beats slow, metronomic, fluttering softly,
like muffled clapping, or cards shuffling. Superb at soaring.
So oddly, but effectively designed, these graceful dirigibles—
like those heavy jets that ferry armored cars or equipment—
seem too heavy to fly.

Over the week there's more wing-flapping.
Perhaps it's growing too hot out on the rocks,
or the fish are gone after spawning.
Groups circle overhead like beneficial angels
and their numbers shrink until they're countable,
leaving only a few pair to haunt the lake
and the Mississippi that runs through it,
enough to make kayakers and fishermen look skyward
and ask: *Are those pelicans?*

What shall I call them? A Visitation of pelicans.
A Feast of pelicans. A Wow of pelicans.
An Ecstasy of pelicans. A Transience of pelicans.
And why do they stir me so?
They're like anything beautiful, strange, or rare,
like anything you didn't even know you were waiting for
that's finally arrived.

Crows

I.

Crow Child

In his morning rail-strut,
I see his feet up close:
a child wearing Mother's clunky shoes.

Is his pride a cover for chagrin
at such wiry, clown feet?
The ground is not his element.

II.

Walking Past the Gathering Tree

> *Often as we were leaving we would see a long line of cattle like black lace against the sunset sky.*
> —Georgia O'Keeffe

The past six winters,
I've passed that tree and watched crows gathering.
I've been searching for a way to describe them
the way Georgia did.
Apt, because it surprises, with cattle heavy, and lace delicate.

I have to get sight, sound, and feeling into one description:

Trees thickening with crows, braided with crows,
larded with crows, rendered with crows.
Trees tendering crows,
crows peppering trees in autumn's dusk.

Gathered as if summoned to a crow party,
sounding like hard rain against a window.
Black tree-buds waffling in the wind,
broccoli florets on a giant stalk,
flags waving in a used car lot,
cilia in the lungs' bronchi.
Masses of crows in trees like some
elemental process: cells gathering,
reproducing before they split.

The trees, clotted with crows,
call out as one intense, determined, congregation.

Untitled

The Rhododendron:
crepe paper flowers. and leaves
like the hands of clowns.

Nest

I found a cunning nest resting on the ground,
woven of soft grasses and pieces of birch bark.
So small, it could fit in the palm of a child's hand.
The wind must have knocked it from a tree.

Though woven of soft grasses and silver slivers of bark,
despite the impact, it was unharmed.
The wind must have jolted it from the tree.
I hope the hatchlings fledged before it fell.

Despite its roughing up, the nest was still intact.
I handed it to a child to hold for me
wondering aloud, what birds were launched before it fell.
So soft, so perfectly constructed.

So I could take a photo, the child held it for me,
this mosaic made of pieces of strewn things—
a useful art—cuplike, entirely constructed
like this poem—of something found on the ground.

Petoskey Stones

Before it was a mitten, Michigan was anchored
in a warm shallow sea below the equator
where coral fed on plankton,
their bodies huddled in colonies.

When the sea withdrew, minerals swept in
and transformed the coral communities
into fossils made of calcite, quartz, pyrite.

Slowly, tectonic plates made their move.

Then, glaciers strode over everything,
plucking up hard fossils from bedrock, breaking, flinging,
scattering them like seeds all over Michigan.

Oceans and ice masses, weather and sand
smoothed and rounded their jagged edges,
and when the people finally came,

they called them *Petoskey,*
after the settlement on the big lake named in of honor the father
who—seeing his child for the first time, rays of sun in his face—
called him *Petosegay:* Rising Sun.

Discovered best in early spring after ice
pushes a new crop to shore. Found too,
in ditches, road beds, gravel pits, and rock shops.

Dull-gray and unremarkable when dry,
wet, these coral tombs bloom
into startling honeycombs of stone.

Bent backs aching, eyes smarting, patient ones
find and collect these coral-fossils,
and polish or show them in water-filled bottles
to call attention to their detail.

Each white hexagon contains a dark spot—
once a mouth—now filled with stone.
Despite their silence, these ancient mouths speak
of a raw, untarnished world.

October Bike Ride on the Kal-Haven Trail

A bike club on a tear leaves us in their dust.
We pedal past the funky pig-farm smell,
fields speckled with grazing cows genuflecting to the sun,
the spring green of alfalfa gripping the black soil,
and a picker that grinds and husks
shooting fine corn dust high into the air.

We coast past blurs of joggers,
dog-exercisers, glimpses of
someone in a wheelchair,
two on a tandem,
bikers who've stopped to catch a breath,
hand-holders, skipping children,
and a woman strolling with an old man.

We are privileged to be
so small, between high rows of drying corn.
Against the wind we find all the gradual hills,
and inside our helmets
we hear leaves rustling and heaving
like ocean waves, never quiet.

We are a narrow train
that takes the hills and curves with ease
along this former railroad bed.
Sequestered within a leafy tunnel
we follow a kaleidoscope of shift and focus
that moves with us, moves in us,
and brings us to a world that exists most days,
without our notice.

Meditations on Naming: A Series

> "ineffable effable
> Effanineffable
> Deep and inscrutable singular
> Name."
> —T.S. Eliot

I. Naming Nature

There's the scientific name and the common name,
the long name and the short. And no-name, of course:
burnt potato chip bark suggests a cherry tree,
a dizzying fragrance announces the sycamore—aka the plane tree.

I take pleasure in knowing a breed of dog,
types of wind, names of stars,
and knowing names of the esoteric:
Nissl bodies or *Borborygmus*.

A name can be superfluous, add static, wreck the mystery.
All done. Immutable. Dismissed.
Pigeonholed,
a pinned bug in a glass case.

On the other hand, I delight in knowing
that the bird with the high wavering whistle following us
singing *Old Sam Peabody Peabody Peabody*
is the white-throated sparrow

that yesterday's spiky-haired duck
is the red-breasted merganser,
and that aged turtle stopping mid-path
is wearing her name on her shell: *mossyback*.

II. A Higher Order of Care

A way of remembering what was there.

> Everything files better with a name,
> makes it easier to find again.

You have to confess a sin's name to be forgiven.

Naming's the key that unlocks the door into the problem.

I discovered the name of the tree that generates the aroma
that makes me swoon. It lives somewhere on the tip of my tongue.
     I'll find it again.

After nearly biking over a striped feather,
I carry it home in my saddlebag and look it up.
It turns into a wild turkey and flies away.

> Let me tell you my name. I want you to use it when you call me.
> But know: I am way more than my name.

And when I choose to name my feeling *love*,
it'll mark a moment,   leap a leap,
long for a response   alter everything.

III. Peony Garden Paradox

Here for the annual display,
shall I be connoisseur of shades, oenophile of fragrance?

      A flash of red: who sings that song?
      (It's only polite to know the names of birds,
      like knowing the names of friends.)

Both uncovering and deepening,
the act of naming grants heft, substance,
intimacy.

      Entering the garden, I discover the paradox
      of how naming both draws a line,
      and draws you close.

Today's names hide within petticoats of silken slips and crinolines.
Surrounded by rows and rows of whites, ivories, yellows,
pinks, peaches, magentas, reds, tipped or fringed, with lurid centers,
I choose not to know their varieties.

      Instead

I'll stand in their ineffable atmosphere
to bend and decant each one.
I'll forgo any sense of superiority, any appreciation
of the hybridist who designed them,
the scholars who named them,
because today, all they need to be, is peony.

Hike

Two miles west of Hell, Michigan
we hiked the woods near Gosling Lake
where we marveled at a city of doughy white mushrooms,
spied lacy bracket fungus—
like burnt potato chips growing up a tree—
and found brown button mushrooms
tucked into crevices of decaying trunks.

It was our first walk in the woods
since John's hip replacements.
I wore a sling under my coat for a
broken collarbone. We wielded
walking sticks for careful trudging
up and down the low hills
and through the muddy places.

John didn't mind my stopping to snap photographs,
because it gave us time to rest
(photography, like park benches with views).
The afternoon had started out gray, but
as we continued walking, the clouds parted,
the sun inflamed the yellows and oranges,
and the forest blazed, triumphant.

Snow Opera

Snow sweeps onto the stage: operatic, Wagnerian.
Wave after surging wave breaks in an ocean of storm.

Frozen in place, I listen to the sea of violins, the herd of harps,
watch wind conduct entrances and exits, point where to go,
set tempos.

Like ornamental grace notes, snow
filigrees the tops of trees clotted with squirrel nests
and rags of abandoned wasp retreats, dangling.

Ponderous branches of majestic pines lurch and sway,
like fat, rooted sopranos. Snow's horns blast and blow,
and clumps percuss the roof.

Oboe and piccolo birds find shelter offstage
behind a curtain spun by the sky overnight

Inexorable snow imprints the world with white,
helps me feel for mature trees standing stoically
like a drove of cattle, lowing in chorus.

And when I see a nuthatch in search of winter fare
clinging to suet hung off the backboard's pole,
I spy the hero of this opera.

Igniting Memory

Sputnik

In 1957, my Mother gazed out the kitchen window at night,
scrubbing pots in soapy dishwater, trying to
imprint the moon in her mind,

worrying about damage Sputnik might do.
She envisioned it as a huge, spiny ball,
a land-mine, a blind sea creature.

My Mother took movies of the moon in all its phases.
Later, she posed her children in front of it,
and took pictures with her Brownie camera.

Cleaning out the attic, I found one of those photographs,
with crumpled edges, worn from handling,
but still clear and bright. There I was

sitting on the grassy backyard hill
with my two little brothers,
bony knees encircled by thin arms,
glowing speck in the top right hand corner.

Proof

We dressed in long skirts and bonnets one fall Saturday,
gathered bacon fat from our Mothers,
and built a fire under a metal pot in Mary's yard.

Challenged by a male teacher's remark
that women today are soft compared with those of yore,
we bent to candle-making.

We strung would-be wicks over hot fat,
and dipped and cooled all afternoon,
producing skinny, ivory-colored tapers.

The sun set. Growing cold, Mary walked me home.
A stranger shot us a quizzical look, our aroma no doubt
insulting his nose all the way across the street.

Autumn afternoons and the smell of smoke
never fail to ignite the memory of us
with our seven candles, presented to our teacher.

Frailty

The pew is hard, to remind us to listen.
Peppermint wafts through the air.

I sit behind my Sunday school teacher
and sometime church organist,
whose beige dress complements her blonde hair in the sunlight
streaming through the stained glass windows.
Close enough to touch,
her slender, zippered back is posture perfect.
Her name is Faith.

From the pulpit, black and purple robes flowing,
forehead glistening, black hair and eyebrows
heavy stubble despite the morning shave.
He's been up for hours, finishing his sermon.
He seems to be talking right to me.
His voice penetrates, brings me God's anger.
She quivers, trembles.
His name is John.

One morning over scrambled eggs, my parents reveal
that Faith and John have run away together.
Forsaking the church, her husband, two teenagers, his wife, all his children,
they take her last child; their love-child.
My fork clangs as I lose my appetite
along with faith.

Rumor had it, they did it on the catechism classroom table.
(It had been going on for years.)

A sinner, forced to leave the church, his fate became to drive a Yellow Cab. The homeless at a mission became his flock.

There, he served up blessings with the soup, before resuming the endless search for fares.
What became of her, we never knew.

Rhubarb Days

The prized rhubarb my gang and I would find in fields,
lick and slick through baby teeth,
chew raw like a sour drug, coating
insides with a divine bitter
now grows in our backyard where we planted it.
I have learned to sweeten
and never eat it by itself
anymore.

In our raw rhubarb days, we never knew
of the fantastic seed-pod that appears over night
as if some alien being just dropped in,
with its bulging tea-green head atop a long stalk
blindly shoving its mindless way straight up
from the dense depths of the shaded skirt
like an excited man
wearing a dress.

Mars Summer

It was the summer of Mars, and its unusual proximity to earth.
It was the summer of no mosquitoes, no injuries, nothing lost.

It was the summer of high winds harnessed like wild horses,
that carried us around the island, easily.

It was the summer you caught only one perch, (not counting the
one found on your line after untangling it from the motor).

It was the summer we learned the names of the Jerusalem
artichoke and the NY aster,

and you taught me the way to distinguish between white pines
(five needles)—like a hand, and red ones (only two)—like eyes.

It was the summer we fed leftover hot dogs to the dog, drank beer
instead of scotch, and skipped *Taco Night* to eat together, alone.

It was the summer I figured out I could win almost any solitaire
game with three cheats.

And the summer I read *Harry Potter* and Robert Lowell's
Collected Works.

It was the summer I committed the eagle's cry to memory,
saw the deer with her fawn leap across the road near the high line.

It was the summer of the new bed.
So big, it barely fit in the little room.

It was the first summer since your mother's death.
You found her old comb when we moved the bed.

I found her housecoat and her headscarf.
Her corduroy coat was useful out on the lake in the evening.

It was the summer when your foot broke through the dock on the very last day, and we declared:

Next year will be the summer of the new dock!

It was the summer of living in the present,
and we were filled to overflowing with contentment.

Hanging On

Bikes Locked

Remembering
the way he locked our bikes together
and how he's the only one who's ever done that,
and he's been doing it for nearly thirty years.

Passing the wrapped chain around and through
two sets of wheels, joining the loops together,
threading in the lock. Side-by-side, touching,
our bikes are two aluminum animals.

The first time he locked them, we met for lunch,
he brought me Dorothy Sayer's *Gaudy Night*—
the end of the series where Peter asks Harriet to marry him, again,
and she finally says *yes*—

and the ease he has with bikes,
and his beautiful, mechanical hands,
his quads outlined in his jeans,
the way he leans over, the care he takes.

Bounty

The corn is ready for picking and stripping,
for plunging in the boil with a pinch of salt:
hot and sticky, round and round
go the sweet and salty rows.

Our turned-crimson tomatoes ache
for slicing,
sun-warm, slippery on the tongue.

The blueberries are small, tight, and high,
their wine purple worth the stretch,
a backache, heavy bucket.

Our peaches blush with urgency.
Over the sink we catch juice,
when stones let go of flesh.

We've thrummed long enough in the sun,
gaped in rain that's come and gone.
In just-rightness, darling,
we ripen.

My Husband, and the Installation
of the Cabin Shower

You fought the white-winged dragon,
backed plastic laminate into a corner, inhaled
sawdust smoke, crawled the depths
to wrestle with drains, wedged new knees
and a humbled body into a dark cave,
banged skull and knuckles, wounded arms,
as you drilled irrevocable holes in a watertight cubicle,
glued, screwed down and caulked up what
might leak, hung doors with wayward rollers,
tested one shower head after another
my faithful plumber; and when at last
you turned it on, it was conquered,
and after you shined it till it gleamed, you bestowed it
on your cabin mate, your Princess, your Queen.

Burr Riff

With teeth and thumbs they hitch and stick,
these brown burgeoning burrs, these free-loaders
with prickled bristles, these bearable burdens—
small envelopes that hook to book,
tiny travelers that make you their feet—

while here in winter, I am like
this minute fruit, this stoic seed, this
patient prevailer: thumbing rides,
looking for places to cling,
hanging on for dear life by my teeth.

What Holds

Once again circling the same fishing hole,
I wait for the quick tug, the muscled gleam
but everything's vague and strange,
as if I've never been here before
with no landmark, no buoy, nothing I can point to,
as if I'm a visitor to a former workplace,
or my elementary school, but nothing
feels familiar, everything changed.

Why this perpetual return? Revelation
eludes me like the fish that nibbles, but never strikes.
I reel in—there's resistance on the hook—
but it's always a long string of weeds, a wriggling crayfish,
or what's left of a minnow injured by one that got away.
Never the epiphany of the Big Fish.

Waking I'm compelled to ask: What else has altered?
My gait, my face, my husband, as he grows old with me,
dear friends who turn forgetful, fall ill.

Squinting, I try to make out what holds:
the elephant skin of the water,
white gulls flying up like unfolding handkerchiefs only to
plunge head first, an eagle coasting just below the tree line,
the shore, the sunset, the sun itself, the whole
community of fishermen of which I am a part,
sitting or standing in boats lit by lights that we bring,
still casting, still casting.

For Whatever is to Come

Under a furrowed, mackerel sky—first snow coming—
the November trees undress themselves leaf by leaf
in slow reveal, and stand unguarded,
in wait for whatever comes

like the once-new couple undressing each other—
surprise packages, eager to be stirred by what they find,
button by button, a gentle tug over the head,
a zipper or two—often some trouble with a belt—
an unhooking, loosening

and years later, knowing precisely what they'll find,
they skip the preliminaries, slip under cool sheets
and warm each other in a party that needs no dinner dress,
holding on against the opaque chill roaring toward them.

About the Author

Katherine (Kathy) Edgren grew up in Grand Rapids, Michigan and was first published at the age of seventeen under her maiden name: Kathy Kool. She is retired from a long career as a social worker and administrator, and served for three terms on the Ann Arbor City Council. She is a graduate of the University of Michigan with an A.B and an MSW.

Katherine is the author of the book, *The Grain Beneath the Gloss,* and two chapbooks: *Transports* and *Long Division,* published by Finishing Line Press, and has been published widely. Currently she lives in Dexter, Michigan with her husband, John, and her dog, Bella. A grandparent of four, she is an avid bike rider, hiker, singer in the choir, and gardener of vegetables.

www.ingramcontent.com/pod-product-compliance
Lightning Source LLC
Chambersburg PA
CBHW022014160426
43197CB00007B/424